Be Still My Soul

LAUREN CUMMINS
and JOSEPH CUMMINS

Be
Still
My
Soul

A Catholic Parents' Journey
with a Son Who is Gay

Charleston, SC
www.PalmettoPublishing.com

Be Still My Soul

Copyright © 2023 by Lauren Cummins and Joseph Cummins

First Edition

Hardcover ISBN: 979-8-8229-1971-6
Paperback ISBN: 979-8-8229-1972-3
eBook ISBN: 979-8-8229-1973-0

Table of Contents

Dedication

This book is dedicated to our family, who journeyed with us in writing this book and provided the support we needed to share our truth in hopes that it may bring the Spirit and Peace of Christ to another. It is also dedicated to the millions of men and women who accept their own sexuality each day amidst the hatred and isolation they may experience. May their journey of truth bring them to the heart of Christ.

BE STILL,
MY SOUL BE STILL

Psalm 46:10 "Be still and know that I am God"

Still my soul be still
And do not fear
Though winds of change may rage tomorrow
God is at your side
No longer dread
The fires of unexpected sorrow.

God You are my God
And I will trust in You and not be shaken
Lord of peace renew
A steadfast spirit within me
To rest in You alone.

Still my soul be still
Do not be moved
By lesser lights and fleeting shadows
Hold onto His ways
With shield of faith
Against temptations flaming arrows.

God You are my God
And I will trust in You and not be shaken
Lord of peace renew
A steadfast spirit within me
To rest in You alone.

Still my soul be still
Do not forsake
The Truth you learned in the beginning
Wait upon the Lord
And hope will rise as stars appear when day is dimming.

God You are my God
And I will trust in You and not be shaken
Lord of peace renew
A steadfast spirit within me
To rest in You alone.

Keith & Kristyn Getty. Awaken The Dawn ℗ 2009 Getty Music Label, LLC Released on: 2009-01-01 Producer: Phil Naish Composer: Keith Getty Composer: Kristyn Lennox Composer: Stuart Townend

Preface

Photo by San Photography

"Each life that we encounter is a gift deserving acceptance, respect, and love. The word of God helps us to open our eyes to welcome and love life, especially when it is weak and vulnerable."
Pope Francis Message for Lent, February 2017

It was a Saturday afternoon Skype conversation like any conversation in any other week. Our son was always good at communicating with us once a week through Skype, ever since he had moved out of state. This day seemed like any other, except when we heard him say "I have something I need to share with you." Those words to a parent mean something serious. *"I am gay and have been going through this for a while. I did not choose to be gay. I have been in counseling over the last 8 to 9 months and have come to accept this about me. I just want to be able to live a normal life like everyone else. I am not politically gay. I am not promiscuous. I want to have a family like everyone else and I want to commit to one person. My faith is important to me. I wish the Catholic Church would accept it. But I know that is not going to happen."*

We heard both his peace and his strength, knowing he had not come to this realization easily. Throughout his childhood and adolescence, his thinking has always been careful and methodical. We know he had prayed about it as well. He was moral and lived a Christian life. We knew what his journey to accept his sexuality would mean for him and our family. We told him we loved him, we understood, and we would be there for him.

Here is the story of parents' love for their son and their Catholic Christian spirituality. This book is about fears, tears, joy, prayer, healing, and deepening faith. Most of all, it is about letting go and letting God. Be still my soul!

Chapter 1:

THE JOURNEY BEGINS FOR MOM

1 Samuel 16: 7

The Lord does not see things as you see them. The Lord said to Samuel, People judge by outward appearances. But the Lord looks at the heart.

Coming Out

"I am gay." These three words have powerful implications for a parent, but even more so if you are Catholic. Anyone who is raised with a Christian, Catholic spirituality respects the Church's teaching. Yet, we also understand the Church is not perfect and sometimes may even be responsible for the culture's views of life issues, both positive and negative.

So, where do you start a journey with a son you love and are so proud of, and just happens to be gay? We began with prayer. Where else would we begin other than through prayer and the loving relationship we have with our God and our son.

We have two wonderful sons whom I adore. When our older son moved out of state after college, I felt peaceful and sad. I knew, through prayer, that this move was right for him - - he got the ideal job; but it was so far away. I also did not know he was gay when he graduated from college, nor did he accept or disclose this to anyone; though his younger brother told us later he knew. So, this step far away from home was scary for me and for him as well. Yet, through prayer I was at peace and knew he was being called to that job and that state. Callings do not just happen for religious vocations. I have seen a calling in my own life, my husband's, my mom's, and sons' lives and these callings always bring the fruits of the Spirit, including a true sense of the Lord's peace. When we truly give our lives to the Lord, He leads us to where He wants us to be, and we also know how He wants us to share our gifts. You feel truly alive, knowing the Lord has called you to this place, to this job, or to this person and He is with you throughout this experience bringing you joy, peace, and understanding. Marriages can be callings, so can being called to a certain job or service. This is how laity know their callings. So, I knew somehow this was right for him. He was being called away. But I was also watching a son leave thousands of miles away from home. I missed him and adjusted slowly to his empty room, knowing he would not live back at home.

Photo by-Jeremy Cummins

I prayed daily for both of my sons from the day they were born and even more fervently specifically for my older son when he moved. I had offered the rosary daily for them on the way to work and for their future wives. For three years I asked Mary to intercede so that both sons and future wives could be prepared as a gift of the Father to each other and that they would become spiritually grounded with God always first in their lives. I did not know who my sons' wives would be, but I trusted that through Mary's intercessions, both them and their future wives would be prepared for a life of holiness. Mary was a mother and understood the longings of a mother's heart for her children. Her intercessions as the mother of God would be powerfully joined with my own intercessions for a Christ-centered wife for my sons and a life that served the Lord. I trusted that Jesus would listen. After all, how could He ignore His mother.

When I heard that day that my son was gay, I felt as Jeremiah did and said, "You duped me, Lord. I have prayed fervently to you through your mother's intercession for three years and you provide this for my son?" Yet, as I continued to pray, I wondered if this might not be an answer to my prayers. As my son continued to share his journey, more gifts of the Spirit became evident. He was more at peace, more joyful. During the time of his discernment, he became a Eucharistic minister and Sacristan at his parish. He loved sharing the homilies and Sunday services. Excitement about your spiritual life does not happen unless the Spirit is directing your life. Continued prayer affirmed this for me. *Be still and know…*

Photo by-Lauren Cummins

You would have to know our family to see why I felt this might be an answer to prayers. You see, I would classify us as an all-American Catholic family. We have always loved expressing our spirituality and loved being a family with Christ as the center. We were active in the family program at our parish, made special times each week to celebrate family either through game night or movie time, prayed as a family during the liturgical seasons of Advent and Lent, and went on many hikes and family vacations. We also went to family retreats and both our sons were active in scouting, both becoming eagle scouts. They were also active in the youth ministry program. We had our disagreements like every other family; but we were aware of working against the tendency to hurt each other through disagreements. We began a saying when the boys were young that stayed with us even through the teen years. It was a saying we said to each other at the close of our morning prayers. "I see Jesus in you, I will love and respect you today." I smiled when I heard one of my sons say this to the other when they were arguing as teens. Jesus was walking with us in our journey.

This small, simple statement became for me even more real when our son told us he was gay. Our son's realization that he is gay did not change the reality that Jesus lives in him, nor does it change our love and respect for him. He is gift to us, to others, and was created in God's image. I believed through a continued journey with God through constant and consistent prayer, I began to see through God's grace that He heard my prayers. But his calling and our calling would now be different. We would live a new normal, one that may not be accepted by others. This visibility would be a challenge for me as a mom because I wanted to protect him from all that would hurt him, even the Church. The Church's lack of acceptance for gay relationships was the saddest and hardest piece for me. However, this sadness would soon change as we continued our journey and began to see our responsibility within the Church differently.

My husband was Jesus for me. His patient spirit and loving support brought Christ alive in my life. On those days we prayed together, my tears were many from the beginning of this journey. I would just lift my son to the Father and the tears would begin. I was not saddened by his sexuality but saddened by what he may have to endure. It took several months for my tears to stop. I knew that I was also grieving what a mom looks forward to, being a grandma. Prayer always brought me to peace however, despite the many tears. I knew my son was not abused or battered as others sometimes say is *the reason* for gay sexuality. Our son also affirmed this. I knew through prayer that the Father's love was guiding us. If we cannot trust our prayer, then what or who do we trust? I was faithful in trusting our prayer as we laid our hearts open at His feet.

Through prayer, the Lord was asking me to give my worries, fears, family, and my son over to Him. He did not want me to carry my fears as a burden. I had to trust that

He would take care of our son and bless his life. Eventually, I realized that He was telling me that He loved our son more than we ever could. The prayer I had prayed for over three years was taking on a fresh look, with the same purpose.

Sharing with Others

When our son shared with us that he was gay, we were quiet about it for about a year. He said he would share about his sexuality only if it needed to be shared or when the time came that he would ever meet someone. Eventually, throughout this first year, he began to tell others. He had also met someone with whom he wanted to date. When we met him, we felt our son was blessed. Here was someone who was gentle, kind, giving, sensitive and spiritual and we were happy to see a relationship blossom.

As our son became more comfortable with others knowing, we began to tell family members. My mom was open and sensitive and shared she would continue to pray for a partner. She lived her life with Catholic values that took her beyond the traditional structured church to a deep spirituality. She always attended liturgy, even when she was not feeling well. She shared prayers with many saints and prayed daily for all of us. We called her our prayer warrior. My mother passed away as I began authoring this book. I miss her terribly; she was the one that always provided calm and spiritual wisdom that she learned through her life and through her prayer. There is no doubt that the Father is listening to her as she embraces prayer for us in heaven.

Our younger son was supportive from day one. His acceptance of our older son's sexuality was a true gift. The bonds of brothers are generally strong; but this solidified the relationship, and I was happy knowing they would always be there for each other no matter what. Others in the family were also supportive and accepting. This was true on both sides of the family. Family members even shared that this was the first time they saw our son so happy. I would have to agree. The acceptance of family was a true gift to me, since it continued to build on what prayer had acknowledged. His work colleagues were great, and I began to see why God sent him there. The support he felt from both friends, colleagues, and family would sustain him and become the visible sign of the Love of the Father for him and us.

Chapter 2:

ENDLESS PRAYER AND REFLECTION

Photo by-Jeremy Cummins

As we continued to reflect and pray on the Church and its teachings, questions rose about the Church's outlook upon and responsibility to its population having other innate sexualities. Our conversations with each other were many, particularly as we researched articles in Catholic magazines and newspapers and read articles online from other Christian denominations. Some of these resources provided support and encouragement, others made us feel abandoned and marginalized. We believed the Church needed to reflect on this stance and needed to begin to embrace those it currently marginalizes.

As we read the Unites States Conference of Catholic Bishops, USCCB (2006) statement of homosexuality we saw compassion and oppression. Even the word *inclination* that was used in this statement lends itself to some sort of meaning that connotes a false sense of sexuality, a kind of being there, but not really. "To the extent that a homosexual tendency or *inclination* is not subject to one's free will, one is not morally culpable for that tendency." (6) Was the Church afraid to say sexuality?

Do others also have an *inclination* to be heterosexual, but not really? When I looked up the definition, *inclination* was defined as *a person's natural tendency or urge to act or feel in a particular way*. So, if this is natural what is the issue and why does the Church embrace both compassion and oppression in its' statement? In any case, reading this word was puzzling and to some degree offensive.

We wanted life to be so right for our son. No one wants their children to suffer at the hands of others. Our prayers were directed to the Father, to Jesus and to Mary. Prayer to Mary at this time was so natural and appropriate since she understood what a parent felt when their child suffered at the hands of others. Witnessing suffering at the hands of others is difficult to see and feel. We find it difficult to realize that the Catholic Church hold beliefs that hurt its members and hurt our son. Solace came through prayer and the knowledge that other Christian faiths are beginning to embrace committed, same-sex relationships.

There is no doubt in our hearts and minds that God is at our side. Sexuality is not a choice as some want to believe. Numerous research studies confirm this as a complicated issue with genetic roots. (Hegarty 2002; Bailey and Pillard 1995; Hamer, et al. 1993; Pillard and Bailey 1998; Sanders, et al. 2014; Zietsch 2008) None of us chose to be heterosexual any more than any of us choose to be homosexual. No one outwardly says, "I think I will be gay and embrace the ridicule of others and not be fully accepted by my Catholic faith or others." It is a difficult journey, especially since it connotes that individuals who have a gay sexuality are unhealthy, sinful, and may need to be counseled out of this *inclination*, which points to a degree of dysfunction. All these labels are placed on them by the Catholic Church whose calling is to be a refuge for the marginalized and it is this bias that quietly supports others to marginalize.

We sometimes thought that it would have been so much easier if our son wanted to be a priest. He shared with us that he thought about this when he first accepted his sexuality, but he said he would be running away from life if he did that. He did not feel called to this ministry, even though he knew he would be spared others' judgements. The Church knows that many priests are gay, and we accept this; we do not talk about this as a Church, but we know it is true. Some priests who are gay sometimes condemn others for being in same-sex relationships. The Church will never be fully alive when we hide behind our own reality, while condemning others. We talk among ourselves, priest to priest, and lay person to lay person, but we never discuss this as Church. In 2021, Pope Francis opened a process of listening and dialogue for the Universal Church, named the 'Synod on Synodality.' Scheduled as a period of 'mutual listening' for three years, priests, religious, and laity who have been gathering, first on a local level, then national level, culminating in the universal dialogue in Rome in 2024, to discern what the Holy Spirit is asking the Church to be and to do in these current times. Will the Church emerge as different and changed? It may be a beginning.

The Church would also say that the *inclination* of being gay is in and of itself not immoral. It is being in a relationship that is not accepted and seen as a moral evil, even if that relationship is a committed one. So, the attitude of *you can look, but do not touch* puts on the brakes for any committed relationship. If not given the option for a blessed covenant relationship can sexual drive give-in to selfish sensual pleasure? Denying a covenant, committed relationship appears to be a contradiction of accepting the gift of sexuality that defines a great deal about who we are as human beings. Our sexuality allows us to express an innate desire to freely give love to another. Denying someone's desire for a same-sex relationship or calling others to conversion or reparative therapy, the goal of which is to help an individual *change* their same sex attraction, implies that such attraction is based on some type of past trauma. While the United States Conference of Catholic Bishops remains ambiguous regarding the merits of conversion therapy, there is evidence that this treatment is coming through the back door through healing services that approach homosexuality as a wound caused by some form of trauma that needs to be healed (Damian 2021). We feel this denies the very essence of who that person is created to be. Consider the outcry if the Church forbade heterosexuals from forming committed relationships. Talk to anyone who is gay and listen. You may hear their pain of wanting to live a life of love with someone for the rest of their lives. They understand commitment, fidelity, and love. It is the Catholic Church that does not see this as a reality for a gay couple, wanting them to convert and change to what they believe is normal. But by not accepting this form of covenant relationship, is the Church in some ways encouraging uncommitted relationships that the bible refers to as promiscuous? Conversion therapy in all its forms has not worked and has been an act of abuse in many cases, leaving individuals suicidal and broken (Lapin 2021). My heart feels joy and I feel a degree of parental pride for those who have had the courage to follow their hearts and Christian conscience in committing to another in a covenant relationship.

We are often amazed that the church will marry individuals who have lived together and have never attended Mass because they want a *church wedding*. But the Catholic Church will not bless a committed gay relationship where individuals have attended Mass. Whether the Church calls committed gay relationships a marriage or not is irrelevant. What is relevant is the fact that the Church (USCCB 2006) is unwilling to embrace these committed relationships, welcoming them to be present together to celebrate at liturgy and be involved in the community. There are many marriages that are blessed and not blessed in the Catholic Church that are life-giving. Both heterosexual and homosexual marriages can exemplify *sacrament, the living presence of Christ*, and should be received by the Church as gift!

The Church has also stated that marriages must be open to *procreation*. Is the idea of procreation an excuse? What about heterosexuals who are infertile, or do not want children, or those who are elderly and remarry? If we follow the teaching of the Church should these examples of committed relationships marry? Does the phrase "openness to life" only refer to bearing children? Can some individuals not even be fit to be a parent? We would like to believe that having a child will nurture a person's selfless giving but talk to abused children and see if their parents ever came to this reality. Could it also be possible that not all married individuals are called to be parents?

The issue with marriage within the Church seems to be more than procreation. It appears that the Church sees marriage without procreation as unnatural, almost against human order. In the USCCB (2006) the bishops stated, "Same-gender acts cannot fulfill the natural ends of human sexuality. By its very nature, the sexual act finds its proper fulfillment in the marital bond. Any sexual act that takes place outside the bond of marriage does not fulfill the proper ends of human sexuality. Such an act is not directed toward the expression of marital love with an openness to new life. It is *disordered in that it is not in accord with this twofold end and is thus morally disordered when sought for itself, isolated from its procreative and unitive purposes.*" (3) Is God not so much more than we are able to fully grasp? How does this message of love and compassion transfer to the 21st century, to the countless individuals who are trying to tell us their story? What are the medical and psychological fields telling us related to same-gender attraction? Do we discard studies and individuals' truths to buy into our own ideologies as Catholics? Could it be that same-gender attraction is different and does begin at birth? I believe we must remain open to the Holy Spirit who guides us to deeper ways of God's love. We must believe that Jesus wants to be as transparent to us today as He was when he walked on earth. We must continue to pray that we hear what Jesus and the Holy Spirit say to us. We need to trust what Jesus and the Spirit say to us through laity and experts alike, even if they are not in agreement.

The Father's story of life and love is ever-unfolding. We understand and accept that discernment and a Christ-centered conscience consider knowledge in its many forms. First is the knowledge and understanding of our own faith. Our spiritual journey is formed by our active involvement in Church that includes attending liturgy, being involved in various spiritual activities as retreats, and reading books and theological views on spiritual topics, which in this case is homosexuality. Second, we must be open to other God-guided sources such as medicine and psychology. Finally, we must be open to other individuals who are on the same pilgrimage for knowledge, understanding, and acceptance, along with those from a wider Christian community, help us form a Catholic, Christian conscience that desires to please God and live His will.

In the *Little Black Book, Cycle Six: Six Minute meditations for Lent.* (Untener and Haven 2019) the following statement spoke to remaining open to God's word in its many forms. *The problem is when I see everything and claim that I do…and refuse to open my eyes to what God has to offer.* We must continually remain open to where God is leading us and understand that God speaks through His people. Could the Hierarchy of the Church believe they see everything and know what is right? I remember a similar story about this with the Pharisees, Sadducees, and chief priests during Jesus's time. All the Jewish leadership believed in the truth and finality of their laws. There was no room or margin for change. "Jesus' proclamation of a kingdom in which the unclean is clean and the unlawful is lawful turned inside out just about everything Jews of his time believed, giving a new way of living to many but making much of the leadership hostile—a conflict that led eventually to Jesus' death." (Schorn 2017, par. 7)

I am not aware of any dialogue that has been provided to the gay community by the Catholic Church that would allow them to share their stories. God speaks through His people, if only we would listen. The Synod of 2024 is listening, and His people are speaking. Will there be a refreshing new view of what is needed for marginalized Catholics, or will we allow fear to overcome the Spirit?

I believe that bringing forth life comes in many forms. A love between two committed same-sex individuals, who bring their relationship under God can pro-create life as well, just in a separate and different way, a way that the Church needs. There is also a distinct difference between being homosexual and being promiscuous. Nothing is more powerful than loving another through a committed relationship, through all its struggles and redeeming love that has our Father as the head of this relationship.

I have seen the pow-
er of love in my son's life
as they delivered a pie to
welcome a new neighbor
or delivered cupcakes to a
neighbor who found their
dog. I saw this in my son
when he gives gift cards

Photo by-Jeremy Cummins

during the holiday season to all airline personnel when he
travels or donates to his diocese to provide for the poor. I
see this in his continued love for the Church, the Eucharist, and his Catholic, Christian journey, despite his feelings of rejection. The Spirit is alive in someone when we
see the fruits of the Holy Spirit! God is so much greater
than what we claim we know.

It is difficult for any parent of a child who is gay to
see church leadership stall committed gay relationships. I
believe that men who hold high positions in the Church
and cling to power and prestige are detrimental to the
Church. Absolute power corrupts absolutely. Nevertheless,
the Spirit moves gently through His people to sanctify
what the Church wants to disdain. Catholic movements
such as Future Church (https://futurechurch.org/), Dignity
(https://www.dignityusa.org/), Outreach (https://outreach.
faith), the Reform Project (https://reformationproject.
org/), and Fr. James Martin (2017) seek to provide dignity

to what others feel is shameful and help the marginalized embrace their callings and their sexuality.

Fr. Martin's (2017) book, *Building a Bridge, How the Catholic Church and the LGBT Community Can Enter into a Relationship of Respect, Compassion and Sensitivity* provides a sign to all of us that the Spirit is moving within the Church. I believe that we may be called to be part of the change that the church needs, a church of humility, self-awareness, welcome, and of mercy.

I once heard a priest say in his homily on justice and acceptance that "I have talked many times about not doing harm in any way to those who are gay. We need to accept them. We do not have to like what they are doing, but we must accept them." I sat there in anger and hurt. Does this type of statement promote genuine acceptance, or does it promote animosity and polarization? We love our brothers and sisters from afar and we manage to keep our distance. What a difference it would have made if the priest talked about acceptance and the fact that we are all children of God on a journey. "LGBT people are treated like lepers in the Catholic Church, and it's time for a change" (Martin quoted by Merritt 2017).

How long will it be that the church ignores those that are seen as lepers and are held at bay? How long will we stand in judgement professing what we know others do and should be ashamed? What fears do we carry that allow us to nurture bigotry and hate, stay silent through it all, believing we are doing the right thing? We have had priests celebrate liturgy and celebrate the sacrament of reconciliation while sexually abusing others in private. Yet, some of these are the same priests who say committed relationships of the same sex are judged as a sin. We find so much wrong with this contradiction and wrong with judgements that alienate without listening, that hurt others without being introspective and honest, and who abuse others, using their position in the church to take a harmful stance over the most vulnerable.

We must work together as Church and become honest and ask harder questions. It seems like we are running from who we are. Afraid that we may one day have to look more deeply and internally at ourselves. Yet, the gentle Spirit is calling us to look hard at who we are. We are all on this journey and parents of children who are gay need the Church, our children need the Church, and most importantly, the Church needs them to bring their charisms (that is, the Holy Spirit-given power for the good of the Church) they have been given to make the Church that much richer in the grace and glory of God.

Chapter 3:
A DAD'S JOURNEY

My husband's journey was different than mine. My journey was based on emptying myself to the Father and was flooded with tons of research. From my viewpoint, my husband's journey was based on his faith and his work as a mental health clinician and educator. He was quite familiar with the continuum of human sexuality, and he shared that we all fall somewhere on this continuum. He also knew through his studies, that people do not choose their sexuality (American Psychological Association 2008). He was quite aware of what the sciences are discovering increasingly about genetics, and the role this plays in sexual orientation. He was more self-assured and at peace. We knew that our love for our son was at the heart of our journey, and he was my strength and my counsel when the tears fell. Here is his story.

I recall a full range of emotions the day our son told us he was gay. The field of emotions continued through the following days, months, and years. I was more self-assured and at peace than my wife when I began this journey as a husband and father. My study and work as a mental health clinician and educator afforded me more exposure to LGBTQ issues than she had. However, I would be disingenuous to claim that I have not been subjected to years of societal stereotypes regarding members of this community, and yes, part of what had long influenced my decision to hold these stereotypes was my upbringing and experience as a Catholic. In addition, my upbringing and experience as a Caucasian, heterosexual, cis-gender (gender identity corresponding with the sex I was identified at birth) male also influenced my hold to the stereotypes, and do I dare say, the prejudices against members identifying with LBGTQ identities.

By the time our son came out to us, I was long on my journey of acceptance of the LGBTQ community. The best way to root out our prejudices regarding members of any group is to become exposed to members of that group. From the beginning of my work as a mental health therapist, my assumptions were challenged as I had the opportunity to work with, treat, and befriend members of the LGBTQ community. Having my assumptions challenged yielded a good deal of conflict for me as the awareness my clients provided was initially foreign to me. I found, in time, I have grown to be much more accepting, and beyond that, that my life has been enriched. So that by the time our son came out, I was in a much better spot. Still, I had one immediate concern that I still needed to work through, "What kind of life will our son have, living and relating in a culture that I fear continues to discriminate?"

I thought of the many people I have come to know who have had to confront this reality themselves. I found myself deeply appreciative as they paved the way to make society more open and accepting of LGBTQ individuals. Nevertheless, we are far from the day when we will tolerate, let alone celebrate uniqueness and difference. I feared that our son was beginning a journey that would include many hardships including that he would be the brunt of intolerance, even violence. However, this was a growth moment for me. Why are we not there yet? Why are we not there as a society and more importantly as a Church? I wondered how my own attitudes, behaviors, and assumptions contributed to our not being there yet. What do I need to do?

The first thing I needed to do was to express to our son my full acceptance and love for him. I needed to express empathy for the difficult journey he had been on. I needed to accept the fear, and sadness that I felt because he had been on this journey for some time without his father's support. I had to repent for my part in maintaining a society and church where this is even an issue in the first place.

I am happy that his mother and I were able to immediately communicate our love and acceptance to him on that Skype call. It took a little time, but I waited for when we were alone together, in person, to apologize to him for my role in maintaining the society and church that bemoans difference. I also apologized for ways I communicated my own prejudices regarding being gay over the years. Today, I am immensely proud of our son and how he has embraced himself and who he is in the manner that he has.

Chapter 4:
WHAT RESEARCH TELLS US -MEDICAL AND PSYCHOLOGICAL INSIGHT

Some Christians and Catholics believe that homosexuality is evil and have created an image of someone to be disdained, like the person with leprosy in Jesus's time (Martin 2017). Though it seems contraindicated, the Church must take some responsibility for instilling and supporting these beliefs. Differences can make us uncomfortable and can breed hate. If we are ever to embrace a truly Christ-centered approach to our faith, then we must become honest with ourselves and form our Christian conscience through a pilgrimage of seeking & studying.

We often wonder if the violence we see against a different sexuality is not due in part to the lack of voice from the Church. Though the USCCB (2006) comes out against any violence, the Church stays quiet as others are abused or even murdered, as in the Orlando mass killings. On June

12, 2016, a 29-year-old man killed forty-nine people and wounded fifty-three in a mass shooting at the gay night club, the Pulse in Orlando Florida. The Pope came out with a statement provided by the Holy See press office after this violence. "The terrible massacre that has taken place in Orlando, with its dreadfully high number of innocent victims, has caused in Pope Francis, and in all of us, the deepest feelings of horror and condemnation, of pain and turmoil before this new manifestation of homicidal folly and senseless hatred." (Holy See Press Office 2016). But we personally heard no words of compassion coming from the Sunday liturgies we attended. Did you? What did the rest of us feel about this violence and did we speak out against it?

Some Christians and Catholics may believe that God is showing the victims of sexuality-driven violence that they are sinful, and that the violence is a just punishment. Christ-centered individuals know that this is not true. As the saying goes; "Be the change you want to see." The USCCB (2006) states that we need to become active in the change to prevent harm to those who might be subjected to sexuality-based violence. Silence is part of the problem, so is reparation therapy that *gas-lights* individuals into therapy that consistently badgers them into so called truths (your dad did not love you, you were somehow traumatized) or demonizes their sexuality, treating them as flawed individuals. Should bishops, priests and laity not be declaring that all individuals are children of God? Why are individuals coming out of this therapy suicidal? If rallies, marches, and protests take place concerning abortion, then why not about acts that oppress and kill those with a different sexuality? Can homophobia be a cause of oppression?

The statement by the USCCB (2006) seems no more than providing a $20.00 bill in the collection for the oppressed who are gay. We feel good and feel we have done our part. But the oppressed remain oppressed. Jesus sat and ate with those hated by others. He embraced and healed the leper and chose a hated tax collector as one of His own apostles. His love healed. His acceptance healed. Can we ask less from those who serve in Jesus' name? We believe that Jesus would have addressed this in our day with compassion and acceptance and would not have marginalized or oppressed, nor required reparative therapies.

The statistics paint a clear picture of the sexuality-marginalized community. Myers, Wilson and O'Neill (2021, 3) point out:

- Forty-five percent of LGBTQ adults reported being agnostic, atheist, or "nothing in particular," and the rest (55%) identified with some religion.
- One-third (33%) of LGBTQ people had shifted from the Christian or other organized religious affiliation they had during childhood to become atheist, agnostic, or nonreligious as adults.
- As adults, more than one-third of LGBTQ people had been hit, beaten, or physically or sexually as-

saulted; had been robbed or had property stolen; or had an object thrown at them.

- More than half of LGBTQ people had experienced threats of violence, and approximately 3 out of 4 had been verbally insulted or abused.

In line with the above statistics, Cornell University (2022) provided a review of 300 peer-reviewed studies that looked at the mental health impact that anti-LGBTQ sentiments had on well-being. Two-hundred and six of these studies (95%) found that discrimination was associated with mental and physical health that harm LGBTQ people. Imagine the heartache associated with understanding the pain of isolation, living without community support, and the prospect of violence simply because of your sexuality.

Photo by-Jeremy Cummins

We are all on a journey of a relationship with a loving Father who calls us by name. However, it seems that we deafen His call to those with various sexualities. God is the judge, not us. We are called to invite them to the journey of walking with a faith community who love and support them on their Christian walk. Our dreams, aspirations, hopes, and commitments, all of what makes us human, are no different than those who have a different sexuality. And when we fail to acknowledge this, our biases become strongholds, redefining the Church Jesus intended.

As Catholics who are educators, researchers, and parents, our life decisions are influenced by the Church and by what experts report. We wonder why we are fearful to bring expertise into prayer. We wanted to present in this book to some small degree what others in the Christian family say, what the Church and Pope have to say, and what medicine and psychology have shared. Expert vantage points prevent marginalizing others based on personal biases. We cannot begin to form our conscience and our calling in life until we are open to what the Father has offered us through the gift of others and then bring this back into prayer.

For many of the medical papers and summaries Michael Pepper's and Beverly Kramer's (2015) work summarized it all quite well. Pepper in 2015 was director of the Institute for Cellular & Molecular Medicine at the University of Pretoria in South Africa and Beverly Kramer was Assistant Director of Research and post graduate support in Faculty Health Sciences at the University of Witwatersrand in South Africa. Both are experts from the molecular and biological fields. They stated that "people who are attracted to others of the same sex develop their orientation before they are born. This is not a choice and scientific evidence shows their parents cannot be blamed. Research proving that there is biological evidence for sexual orientation has been available since the 1980s. The links have been emphasized by new scientific research." (par. 1, 2)

South Africa, which criminalizes same sex attraction had experts in their country support those who were not only marginalized, but had extreme intolerance lorded over them. The study panel from the Academy of Science in South Africa (2015) concluded that "there was substantial biological evidence for the diversity of human sexualities and for sexual orientations in particular. Studies have found significant linkage between male sexual orientation and regions of the X chromosome. This particular region on the X chromosome is also associated with other elements of sexual development. These findings, initially published in 1993 and confirmed in 2014, directly associate a particular trait (same-sex orientation) to genetic material for at least some same-sex-attracted men. The mechanisms through which gene expression impacts on sexual orientation remain to be determined. Although less well studied, there is also considerable evidence for a biological component for same-sex orientation in women." (39)

Sullivan (2019) who received his Ph.D. in cell and molecular biology from the University of Pennsylvania and is an award-winning professor at the Indiana University

School of Medicine in Indianapolis, cited that "geneticist Andrea Ganna at the Broad Institute of MIT and Harvard, and colleagues, described the largest survey to date for genes associated with same-sex behavior. By analyzing the DNA of nearly half a million people from the U.S. and the U.K., they concluded that genes account for between 8% and 25% of same-sex behavior. Our genes can influence who we are, and psychologists contend sexual orientation is **not a conscious choice.** It theoretically stands to reason there might be genetic underpinnings to who we become sexually attracted to." (McBride 2021, par.1)

Numerous studies have established that sex is not just male or female. Rather, it is a continuum that emerges from a person's genetic makeup. Modern technologies in DNA sequencing and cell biology are revealing that everyone is, to varying degrees, a patchwork of genetically distinct cells, some with a sex that might not match that of the rest of their body. Some studies even suggest that the sex of each cell drives its behavior, through a complicated network of molecular interactions. Nonetheless, *"misconceptions persist that same-sex attraction is a choice that warrants condemnation or conversion, and leads to discrimination and persecution."* (Ainsworth 2015, 288)

Findings from family and twin studies also support a genetic contribution to the development of sexual orientation. "Research estimates that about 8% of the population is gay, and homosexuality is known to run in families. If one of a set of identical twins is gay, there is a 20% probability that the other will be too" (Norton 2012, par. 2). Norton continues by citing Rice who stated, "homosexuality isn't just a human thing. Among California gulls, which he watched from his office window, about 14% of pairs are female-female. In Australian black swans, some 6% of pairs are male-male, and 8% of male sheep are attracted exclusively to male partners." (par. 3)

In addition, years of research has suggested that individuals cannot change their sexuality (American Psychological Association 2009, 2022; Bishop 2019; Jones et al. 2018; What We Know Project, 2017). Unfortunately, the United States Conference of Catholic Bishops never clearly came out with a statement in 2006 that discouraged therapies and treatments that did not honor the conscience formation of the individual and honor their giftedness as a child of God. It is important to note that an understanding of homosexuality as a normal variant of human sexuality is currently taken as the basis for the ethical stance of many professional organizations including both the World Medical Association (2013; Mahler and Mundle 2015) and the World Psychiatric Association (Bnugra et al. 2017). A scientific understanding of this variation helps to clarify the basis for that ethical stance. (Cook 2021)

We find it interesting though, that the Church who calls all of us to respect and accept each other as children of God implies that these children need to change themselves as if they were damaged. Researchers believed that therapeutic treatments that come from the perspective that same sex attraction is a mental disorder are wrong and create harmful stereotypes. These treatments deny actual data and can reinforce and sustain negative stigmas, along with denying health development for the individual (Haldeman 2002; Shidlo and Schroeder 2002; Beckstead and Morrow 2004; Lilienfeld 2007; Lapin 2021).

Chapter 5:

WHAT THE CHURCH TELLS US- "HOMOSEXUAL INCLINATION"

Now, what about our Catholicism? We, as well as our sons, are rooted in our Catholic faith. We have shared several ways we have worked consciously to nurture faith and Catholicism with our sons including prayer, attending liturgy, going to faith-based experiences like retreats, and spending time reading publications that nurture our spiritual growth. We still embrace our faith, even though in some circles, our son's capacity for intimacy is 'objectively disordered,' (USCCB 2006). What keeps us Catholic? Many Christian denominations are much more open and welcoming to LGBTQ individuals, but we remain Catholic. We believe this is because our faith is centered around the Eucharist. Our son cherishes the Eucharist. He has engaged in a parish community where he lives, serves as a Eucharistic Minister and Sacristan. Leaving the Church is not something we want to pursue. WE ARE THE CHURCH! We are the Community of Christ, centered on the Eucharist. As members of the Body of Christ, our role is to transform the Church.

In addition to the centrality of the Eucharist, several other features of Catholicism draw us to our faith. First, the Church's mission is to be a sacrament of God's love in a broken world. Activities that support this mission are based on the teaching of Christ focused on demonstrating love and concern for the poor and disenfranchised. Countless followers of Jesus (both local individuals and the Church Institution) embrace this aspect of the mission and we are drawn to the Social Justice teaching of the Church. Over the years, and certainly today, the Catholic Church has been criticized for its prophetic voice, crying out for justice, especially for the poor and disenfranchised, the Church's teachings regarding abortion, the death penalty, immigration, etc.

The Church, being a community of sinners, also has a history of not fully living up to its mission. History reveals periods and factions in the Church which demonstrated the opposite of what Christ taught such as colonialism, antisemitism, clericalism, and misogyny. All of these are rooted in sin and sustained in part by faulty understandings or by the Church's need to justify the status quo of power, wealth, and prestige.

Recently the Church has begun to recognize the sins of the past. In 2022 Pope Francis made a pilgrimage of repentance to Canada, seeking atonement for the Church's role in atrocities experienced by the First Nations people of Can-

Photo by-Jeremy Cummins

ada. Will a future Pope address members of the LGBTQ community expressing similar sentiments for the discrimination and hostility fostered by the Catholic Church?

When Pope Francis was asked by Fr. Martin (America, 2022) what he would tell those who are LGBT he stated, "God is Father, and he does not disown any of his children. The style of God is closeness, mercy and tenderness. Along this path you will find God." (par. 4) In many ways, Pope Francis has opened the Church's heart to the marginalized, including those of the LGBTQ community. He has shared tender thoughts of what the church's responsibility is. The Pope advised the LGBTQ community to view negative experiences in the church not as rejection by the institution but as unfortunate encounters with individuals.

However, it is difficult to reconcile these statements with the Church's continued stance that members of the LGBTQ community are "objectively disordered." (Catechism of the Catholic Church 2000; USCCB 2006) There is a significant disconnect with the hierarchy stating that

LGBTQ individuals are children of God, whom God would never disown; and then stating that LGBTQ individuals have an inclination that is objectively disordered and that any sexual expression is intrinsically immoral and contrary to natural law. This teaching justifies discrimination of individuals who are already subject to such discrimination, both within the Church and society.

One might argue that the Church's contradictory doctrine described above compromises the Church's standing as a champion of justice. What authority can the Church claim as a beacon of social justice when the U.S. Conference of Catholic Bishops (USCCB) has not issued support for the Equality Act that would add sexual orientation and gender identity to the federal civil rights protections that currently exist based on race, color, religion, sex and national origin? Furthermore, the Church finds itself at odds with employment non-discrimination laws, for fear that the Church could be accused of discrimination for unfair employment practices toward LGBTQ individuals.

We maintain hope that under the Spirit's guidance, the Church will revisit this doctrine. Meanwhile, we call upon the Church to develop a more pastoral teaching and dialogue with the LGBTQ community. Living with Martin's (2017) concept of respect, compassion, and sensitivity for the LGBTQ community should call for an outcry against any form of discrimination or violence against LGBTQ individuals. Fr. Martin's (2017) traits would result in accepting the science-based recognition that homosexuality is not just a deep-seated inclination but rather an innate expression of sexuality. Martin's traits should result in tolerance for and a celebration of differences that weave the fabric of humanity ordained by God.

Several organizations raise the dignity of homosexuality and celebrate and embrace this difference as we have mentioned earlier. Three of them that we are personally aware of are the Catholic organization called Dignity, the Catholic website Outreach, and the Reform Project. The Reform Project is one that touched our hearts since it is an inclusive membership of Catholic, Protestant, and Orthodox Christians who feel it is their calling to support a more welcoming and inclusive church. The Reform Project challenges the Church to be less complicit to, and more outraged by the tragedy of prejudice, discrimination, even violence so often displayed in our society toward the LGBTQ community.

The Reform Project offers several statements that support same-sex relationships. One of the statements on their website spoke a bit differently about the interpretation of scripture related to how homosexuality is discussed. They say that to be "faithful to Scripture, we must recognize a distinction between the same-sex behavior the Bible condemns and the desires of LGBTQ Christians for love, companionship, and family today." (9) Most of the Scripture's condemnation addresses promiscuity between same-sex partners as well as heterosexual partners.

Members of the Reform Project point out that Christian teaching should bear good fruit, not bad. Beliefs that do not affirm same-sex relationships cause Christians, including Catholics to inflict mental and physical harm to those who are LGBTQ. Some of this harm is blatant such as parents rejecting their LGBTQ child, or nations who criminalizes same-sex relationships, often not criticized by the bishops of that nation. Other harm is done covertly by staying silent when others need affirmation and support. "From the inclusion of Gentiles in the church to the abolition of slavery, the church has a long history of revisiting the biblical text in light of compelling evidence that prevailing interpretations do not align with Jesus's teaching in Matthew 7 that good trees bear good fruit." (The Reform Project, par. 1)

"The Bible honors celibacy as a worthy calling, but it also makes clear that celibacy is a gift that not all have (1 Corinthians 7:7-9, Matthew 19:11). Requiring that all gay Christians remain celibate for life because of their sexual orientation is at odds with the Bible's teachings on celibacy" (The Reform Project, par. 3). So why then are same-sex partners encouraged to form what the Church would refer to as celibate friendships, regardless of the gift?

In addition, The Reform Project highlights the fact that nowhere in Scripture does it state that marriage is a calling that has procreation as its central piece. The Reform Project identifies the primary focus of marriage as a covenant, which is to be a reflection of the relationship between Christ and his church (Ephesians 5:21-33). A covenant is a holy commitment of love and faithfulness. "Christian same-sex couples live out this covenant every day, often through experiences and environments that are hostile and challenge the very essence of who they are. But they maintain, cultivate and sustain this love" (The Reform Project, par.10). We wonder how many heterosexual relationships could maintain this type of commitment amidst these hostile experiences. "The general framework for thinking about sexual morality should not be determined by generalized condemnations of undefined behavior." (Outreach, par. 24) Our sexual ethics should be grounded in the command to love.

Chapter 6:
WHAT OUR GOD TELLS US

Photo by-Jeremy Cummins

Psalm 46:10
Be Still and know that I am God.

This scripture continued to have a resounding impact on our lives as we journeyed with a new understanding of family. We attended our first Catholic retreat for the LBGT community around three years after our son shared his sexuality with us and attended another retreat after COVID. The retreats reminded us to *Be still and know that I am God*, a God who loves us and ordains our destinies from the beginning. It reminded us to celebrate our journey together with a loving Father.

The retreats continued to affirm the suffering that committed gay couples endure. Through many of the small group experiences we heard stories from men just wanting to be a part of their faith community and of a Church who denied them this reality. We heard stories and experiences of rejection and scorn. This rejection was difficult to hear, since most of the stories from these men were about their experiences of rejection from the Catholic Church community. We sat in sadness and anger as we heard stories that tore into our hearts and affirmed that as a Church we are not as welcoming as we profess. The dichotomy between what the Church preaches and what it practices became clear. We heard from Scripture that our God does not judge as humans judge and knows our hearts with an enduring and endless love. All these men, women, and parents in attendance are endowed with gifts and talents that need to be shared within the Church. We felt ashamed for the first time that our Church has been a part of so much anguish and guilt laid on the shoulders of those who did not choose this destiny but accepted it as a calling to live the life they were meant to live.

The Catholic Church holds that homosexual individuals be "accepted with respect, compassion, and sensitivity."

(Catechism of the Catholic Church 2000, 566) In Catholic churches around the country, parishioners are taught to avoid demonstration of 'unjust' discrimination against members of the LGBTQ community, (though this is not promoted in all Catholic parishes). Yet, while the Church attempts to portray a pastoral acceptance of LGBTQ individuals, committed relationships are forbidden in the Church. The Catechism of the Catholic Church, (2000) names homosexual acts as "intrinsically immoral" and "contrary to natural law" (566). It is hard for any parent who knows their child to believe their sexuality is intrinsically immoral while the reality of *science* tells us that homosexuality is not a choice, just another normal. We felt anger and betrayal from our Church.

In the movie series, *The Chosen* created and directed by American filmmaker Dallas Jenkins (Loaves and Fishes Productions, Angel Studios and Out of Order Studio, 2022), Nicodemus asked a Pharisee that he mentored; "If God did something outside of the Torah, would you question God, or would you question your interpretation of the Torah?" That line from Nicodemus to another Pharisee touched our hearts, since it spoke to our journey as parents of a gay son. If we are called to witness to a calling that Church does not fully embrace, is it possible that God is speaking? It is often in our daily journey that the Father so lovingly continues to affirm the journey. "Be part of the change, you want to see."

God continues to affirm that our son and his partner are in the palm of His hands. He promises He will not abandon us, will not betray us, remains steadfast in His love, and will continue to be our support, even though the Church might not. He has shared in so many ways through conversations with others that HE is the only one that we are accountable to, and no one can claim they know the Father when they harbor inner hate and disgust for another. We are journeying on His wings, His strength, His direction, and His calling. We have walked with others in the Church who have this same calling and we are all witnesses to the fact that this journey must be accepted and embraced by the Church if they genuinely believe in embracing the marginalized.

This book is all about prayer, love, trust, spirituality. It is about a journey that we took together. We did not look for research or organizations to convince us we are OK. We sought to form our Christian conscience about an issue that was near and dear to us and through it all, repeatedly, the Father revealed just how much He loved us, delighted in us, and shares the journey with us. The fruits of the Spirit are alive in our lives because of our great journey that brought everything at the feet of Jesus.

We are slowly discerning how the Father wants us to witness and support other parents in their journey. This quest is in His Hands. We have met others in our workplace who also have children who are gay. All these parents but one, were accepting and supportive of their children. Some have close relationships; others have strained ones. Listening and empathizing are the gifts we can give to others who are hurt and marginalized. We can only be a presence of the Love the Father has for them and be for them a small part of the greater Catholic community.

We wait upon the Lord and thank Him for His ever-loving presence in every moment of our lives. As we continue to journey, we know that God will continue to reveal through Jesus our paths and we know He will for your life as well.

Chapter 7:
I WANT YOU TO MEET SOMEONE

Photo by-Jeremy Cummins

As life continues, we communicate with our son weekly. We are grateful for social media that allows us to talk and see him regularly. Our son shared one day that he was dating someone. He brought him home for Christmas that year and we fell in love with him. This man's genuine care for our son, us, and the rest of our family was quite apparent. He is not Catholic. Our son hoped one day he would become Catholic, but his partner asked," Why do you want me coming into your church if they do not accept us?" This was a hard question to answer for our son and for ourselves. We know that our son wants to share his faith, his spirituality, and love of the Church. He has accepted the Church right now as it is and maintains his own personal journey as a Catholic Christian. However, his longing for this shared spirituality will not go away. How sad that another individual is turned off by a church and remains distant from a community who should provide acceptance for him. Our son's husband is spiritual in his own way, but sad that a church community rejects their relationship and, each of them.

When we met our now son-in-law for the first time at Christmas, we automatically understood why our son was falling in love with him. His tenderness, compassion, and respectful disposition was unfathomable. When children bring home someone for their parents to meet for the first time, the visit can be quiet, sometimes even awkward till you grow to know this person. This first encounter, however, was different. It seemed like we had known him for years. He fit right in and even offered to do the vacuuming during his stay. He was able to meet our son's grandma months before she passed away, which was a true blessing.

Their relationship continued to blossom, and our son and his partner are now married. The minister for their wedding had to have been the most spiritual minister we have met. He shone with a simple faith that was both welcoming and healing. He exuded acceptance and grace and asked all of us to be a true Christian community when he said, "This love has been called forth. Both young men and their relationship will need all your support. Are you all willing to support them?" All the one hundred plus people said, "Yes!" A Christian community born outside of the traditional Catholic church!

In some ways the journey that began with a lot of tears and fears ended with joyful smiles, applause, and laughter. We had no doubt that our son chose the path for which he was destined. His gift of love to his new husband is joy-filled and love-filled. They are both family-focused and look outward together to serve others. They are both the most genuine of people supporting each other and challenging each other to grow. Our son remains faithful to his spirituality and the fruits of this have remained evident. They are on a journey like all of us - - a journey of life, of love, of hurt, and sorrows. They have given their lives to a God who is bigger than all of us. One day they will meet all of you in heaven and continue this story with you!

Epilogue:
THE GOD OF THE IMPOSSIBLE

Photo by-Jeremy Cummins

As I sit here today, concluding the book, I wonder to myself if this will ever be published. I know I felt called to it and talked to my husband, asking him to join in writing it. I have therefore, left this in God's hands. I also know there will be some who read this and will become angry and wonder how we dare challenge the Church and remain Catholic. We did not write this for approval or for anyone to agree, we wrote this as a calling from our hearts to share a journey of the heart! If it challenges you, speak to God about it! If it inspires you, thank the Lord!

The spirituality that we both have developed through our Catholic journey has been a gift to us that hopefully will become a gift to others. More than ever, we believe that each one of us must form their own Christian conscience and be open to hearing what others share, taking all things into prayer or we will become a church where abuse can and will continue to occur, even if this abuse is seen and identified as holy. We have seen this in the way the Church treated the Native American as savage, we still can see the graves where innocent children were beaten to get the evil savage out of them. We see pulpit endorsements of presidents that demonstrate anything but holy, and we see a church (inclusive of all Christian denominations) silent in the face of great discrimination that causes suicides and physical harm.

So, all we know is that we leave our journey in the hands of God. If this book frees one parent from the burden of guilt to find peace in the arms of our Father, then the book has done its job! For now, we continue our journey in hope that one-day, the Church will realize that structures and laws are there to bring people closer to God, that when we abuse this and allow structure to support the "haves" at the cost of the "have nots" we are heading in the wrong direction!

God is faithful, and we are reading and hearing the church's awakenings. Do we really know Jesus in the way he chooses to reveal himself? We are all on a journey of faith and love…it is better to join hands in this journey than to go on this journey as self-righteous individuals who ignore the planks in our own eyes. Let God be the Father and let all of us, help each other along the journey!

May peace reign in your hearts, a peace that only the Father can give! Be Still My Soul and Know that I Am God!

....

Still my soul be still
Do not forsake
The Truth you learned in the beginning
Wait upon the Lord
And Hope will rise as stars appear
when day is dimming!

....

References

A

Ainsworth, Claire. 2015. "Sex Redefined."
Nature 518, no.7539: 288-291.

Academy of Science in South Africa. 2015.
*Diversity in Human Sexuality- Implications for
Policy in Africa.* Pretoria, South Africa.

American Psychological Association. 2008. "Understanding
Sexual Orientation and Homosexuality." https://
www.apa.org/topics/lgbtq/orientation

American Psychological Association. 2009. *Report of
the American Psychological Association Task Force on
Appropriate Therapeutic Responses to Sexual Orientation.*
Task Force on Appropriate Therapeutic Responses
to Sexual Orientation. https://www.apa.org/pi/
lgbc/publications/therapeutic-resp.html

American Psychological Association. 2022. *Resolution on
Appropriate Affirmative Responses to Sexual Orientation
Distress and Change Efforts. (Updated June 2022).*

America. 2022. "Pope Francis Speaks to LGBT Catholics
in New Letter: God Does Not Disown Any of
His Children." *America: The Jesuit Review.* (May 9).
https://www.americamagazine.org/faith/2022/05/09/
pope-francis-james-martin-outreach-242952

B

Bailey, Michael and Richard Pillard. 1995.
"Genetics of Human Sexual Orientation." *Annual Review of Sex Research*, 6(1), 126-150.

Beckstead, A. Lee and Susan Morrow. 2004. "Mormon Clients' Experiences of Conversion Therapy: The Need for a New Treatment Approach." *The Counseling Psychologist*, 32, 651-90.

Bishop, Amie. 2019. "Harmful Treatment: The Global Reach of So-Called Conversion Therapy." New York: Outright International. https://outrightinternational.org/sites/default/files/2022-09/ConversionFINAL_Web_0.pdf

Bnugra, Dinesh, and Kristen Eckstrand, Petros Levounis, Anindya Kar, and Kenneth Javate. 2017. "Gender Identity and Same-Sex Orientation, Attraction, and Behaviors." (October) Position Statement; World Psychiatric Association. https://www.wpanet.org/_files/ugd/e172f3_2842912d737742fdb5d549d2b7ebfc5c.pdf

C

Catholic Church. 2000. *Catechism of the Catholic Church (2nd ed.)*. Catechism of the Catholic   (usccb.org)

Cook, Christopher. 2021. "The Causes of Human Sexual Orientation." *Theology and Sexuality*, 27:1, 1-19. doi: 10.1080/13558358.2020.1818541

Cornell University. 2022. "What Does the Scholarly Research Say About the Effects of Discrimination on the Health of LGBT People?" https://whatwekno.w.inequality.cornell.edu/topics/lgbt-equality/what-does-scholarly-research-say-about-the-effects-of-discrimination-on-the-health-of-lgbt-people/

D - H

Damian, Chris. 2021. "My Diocese's Seminarians Went Through Conversion Therapy, and Didn't Know It." (October 20). http://chrisdamian.substack.com/p/my-dioceses-seminarian-went-through

Dignity USA. https://www.dignityusa.org/

Future Church. https://futurechurch.org/

Haldeman, Douglas C. 2002. "Gay Rights, Patient Rights: The Implications of Sexual Orientation Conversion Therapy." Professional Psychology: Research and Practice 33. 260-264.

Hamer Dean H. and Stella Hu, Victoria L. Magnuson, Nan Hu, Angela M. l. Pattatucci. 1993. "A Linkage Between DNA Markers on the X Chromosome and Male Sexual Orientation." *Science*, 261:321–332.

Hegarty, Peter. 2002. "It's Not a Choice, It's the Way We're Built: Symbolic Beliefs About Sexual Orientation in the US and Britain." (May). https://doi.org/10.1002/casp.669

Holy See Press Office. 2016. "Horror and Condemnation of the Massacre in Orlando, New Manifestation of Homicidal Folly and Senseless Hatred." *Summary of Bulletin*. (June). https://press.vatican.va/content/salastampa/en/bollettino/pubblico/2016/06/13/160613c.html

J

Jones, Timothy W., Anna Brown, Lee Carnie, Gillian Fletcher, and William Leonard. 2018. *Preventing Harm, Promoting Justice: Responding to LGBT Conversion Therapy in Australia.* Melbourne: HRLC & GLHV. https://www.hrlc.org.au/reports/preventing-har

L - P

Lapin, John, J. 2021. "The Legal Status of Conversion Therapy." *Georgetown Journal of Gender & the Law.* https://www. law.georgetown.edu/gender-journal/wp-content/uploads/ sites/20/2021/08/Legal-Status-of-Conversion-Therapy.pdf

Lilienfeld, Scott O. 2007. "Psychological Treatments That Cause Harm. Perspectives on Psychological Science." *A Journal of the Association for Psychological Science* vol. 2,1: 53-70. https://doi.org/10.1111/j.1745-6916.2007.00029.x

M-N

Mahler, Lieselotte and Goetz Mundle. 2015. "A Need For Orientation: The WMA Statement on Natural Variations of Human Sexuality." International Review of Psychiatry 27: 460-462.

Martin, James S.J. 2017. *Building a Bridge; How the Catholic Church and the LGBT Community Can Enter Into a Relationship of Respect, Compassion, and Sensitivity.* Harper Collins; New York: New York.

McBride, Katie. 2021. "The Science of Sexual Orientation. Can Genes Explain Sexuality? Should we even try to know?" *Inverse.* https://www.inverse. com/mind-body/the-science-of-sexuality

Myers IIan. H. and Bianca. D. M. Wilson, Kathryn O'Neill. 2021. "LGBTQ People in the US: Select Findings From the Generation and TransPop Studies." (June). UCLA School of Law, Williams Institute.

Norton, Elizabeth. 2012. "Homosexuality May Start in the Womb: DNA Modifications May Explain How Sexual Orientation is Passed Down Through

Generations." *Science.* (Dec.11). https://www.science.
org/content/article/homosexuality-may-start-womb

O - P

Outreach: An LGBTQ Catholic Outreach.
https://Outreach.faith

Pepper Michael, S. and Beverley Kramer. 2015. "The
Science Behind a More Meaningful Understanding of
Sexual Orientation." *The Conversation.* (June 10). https://
theconversation.com/the-science-behind-a-more-
meaningful-understanding-of-sexual-orientation-42641

Pillard, Richard C., and J. Michael Bailey. 1998. "Human Sexual
Orientation Has a Heritable Component." *Human Biology*,
70(2), 347–65. http://www.jstor.org/stable/41465642

Pope Francis. 2017. *Holy Father's Message for Lent
2017.* Summary of Bulletin. Holy See Press Office.
(February). https://press.vatican.va/content/salastampa/
en/bollettino/pubblico/2017/02/07/170207b.html

Merritt, Jonathan. 2017. "This Vatican Advisor is
Moving Catholics Towards LGBT Inclusion."
Religion News Service. (June 6). https://religionnews.
com/2017/06/06/this-top-vatican-official-is-quietly-
moving-catholics-toward-lgbt-inclusion

R - S

Sanders, Alan R., Eden R. Martin, Gary Beecham, Shengru
Guo, Khytam Dawood, Gerulf Rieger, Judith A. Badner,
et al. 2014. Genome-wide scan demonstrates significant
linkage for male sexual orientation. *Psychological Medicine*,

Vol. 45, Issue 7. (November 17). Cambridge University Press. https://www.cambridge.org/core/journals/psychological-medicine/article/abs/genomewide-scan-demonstrates-significant-linkage-for-male-sexual-orientation/864518601436C95563EA670C5F380343

Schorn, Joel. 2009. "Who Were the Pharisees, Sadducees, and Chief Priests?" *U.S. Catholic.* Vol. 74, No. 3, (March). 41.

Shidlo, Ariel, and Michael Schroeder, M. 2002. "Changing Sexual Orientation: A Consumer's Report." *Professional Psychology: Research and Practice,* 33, 249–259.

Sullivan, Bill. 2019. Stop calling it a choice: Biological factors drive homosexuality. *The Conversation.* (September 3). https://theconversation.com/stop-calling-it-a-choice-biological-factors-drive-homosexuality-122764

T - Z

The Reform Project. 2022. P.O. Box 191013 Dallas, TX. 75219 https://reformationproject.org/case/1-corinthians-and-1-timothy/

United States Conference of Catholic Bishops (USCCB). 2006. *Ministry to Persons with a Homosexual Inclination: Guidelines for Pastoral Care United States Conference of Catholic Bishops.* (November 14). https://www.usccb.org/committees/laity-marriage-family-life-youth/homosexuality

Untener, Ken and Catherine Haven. 2019. *Little Black Book, Cycle Six: Six Minute Meditations for Lent. Little Books:* Diocese of Saginaw, Inc.

What We Know Project. 2017. "What does the scholarly research say about whether conversion therapy can alter sexual orientation without causing harm?" Ithaca: Center for the Study of Inequality, Cornell University. https://whatweknow.inequality.cornell.edu/

World Medical Association. 2013. *WMA Statement on Natural Variations of Human Sexuality*. https://www.wma.net/policies-post/wma-statement-on-natural-variations-of-human-sexuality/

Zietsch, Brendan P., Katherine I. Morley, Sri N. Shekar, Karin J. H. Verweij, Matthew C. Keller, Stuart Macgregor, Margaret J. Wright, Michael Bailey, and Nicholas G. Martin. 2008. "Genetic Factors Predisposing to Homosexuality May Increase Mating Success in Heterosexuals." *Evolution and Human Behavior*. Volume 29; Issue 6, 424-433. https://doi.org/10.1016/j.evolhumbehav.2008.07.002

9 798822 919716